World Crafts and Recipes

Recipe and Craft Guide to

JAPAN

Juliet Haines Mofford

Mitchell Lane

P.O. Box 196
Hockessin, Delaware 19707
Visit us on the web: www.mitchelllane.com
Comments? email us: mitchelllane@mitchelllane.com

Mitchell Lane

World Crafts and Recipes

The Caribbean • China • France• India • Indonesia
• Israel • Italy • **Japan** • South Africa

**Library of Congress
Cataloging-in-Publication Data**

Mofford, Juliet Haines.
  Recipe and craft guide to Japan / by Juliet
Haines Mofford.
    p. cm. — (World crafts and recipes)
  Includes bibliographical references and
index.
  ISBN 978-1-58415-933-9 (library bound)
  1. Cookery, Japanese—Juvenile literature.
2. Handicraft—Japan—Juvenile literature. I.
Title.
  TX724.5.J3M66 2010
  641.5952—dc22

                                              2010008951

Printing   3   4   5   6   7   8   9

                                        PLB / PLB2 / PLB2

CONTENTS

Japan—a group of islands in the Pacific Ocean with a landmass smaller than the state of California—is home to more than 127 million people. Most Japanese live on the four largest islands of Honshu, Kyushu, Shikoku, and Hokkaido. Fifteen million people live in the crowded capital, Tokyo. Nearly 85 percent of the country is too mountainous for farming, and half of the arable land is used for raising rice. With such scarce farmland, much of Japan's food must be imported.

Although a great deal of Japan's culture originated in China, the Japanese became fearful of foreign domination and shut their country off from the rest of the world for two centuries. From 1192 until 1869, shoguns or military warlords, served by loyal samurai, held the political power. Emperors, then considered direct descendents of the Sun God, were honored figureheads rather than rulers. In 1854, the United States Navy, under Commodore Matthew Perry, opened the country to international trade. Japan was soon modeling its educational system, rapid industrialization, and popular culture on those of America and Europe. Japan's lack of natural resources and desire for expansion led to a military coup in the 1930s and soon after to World War II. Following the country's defeat and occupation by American forces, the Japanese people made a firm commitment to democracy. Japan is now respected throughout the world for technological expertise, economic leadership, and devotion to education and art.

The traditional and the modern exist side by side in Japan. Although kimonos are worn only on special occasions and holidays nowadays, most Japanese businessmen still prefer to exchange their Western suits for kimonos when they get home from work. Geta, or wooden clogs, are often worn with Western clothing. The floors of Japanese homes may still be covered with tatami mats, but a carpeted Western room is considered essential for entertaining, and chopsticks are set next to forks on the dinner table.

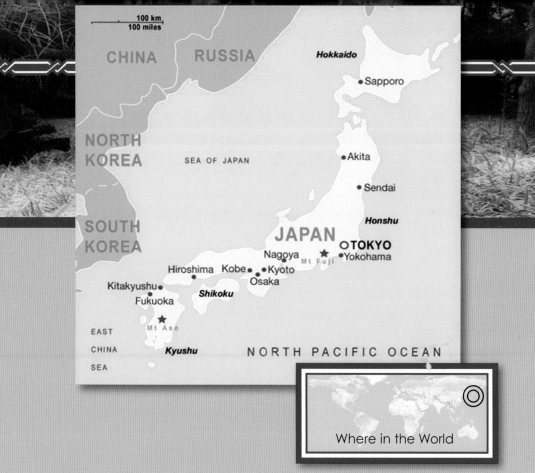

Where in the World

Tastes are changing. Cold cereal and coffee are almost as popular for breakfast as rice and miso soup. Baseball is Japan's national sport, and Christmas and Halloween are celebrated. Young people wear jeans, streak their black hair with bright dye, play Nintendo games, and are seldom without iPods and cell phones. And they frequently meet their friends at *Makudonarudo* under the Golden Arches. Contemporary Japanese prefer their country be known for producing quality cameras, televisions, transistors, and cars rather than as the Land of Cherry Blossoms, geisha girls, and tea ceremonies. Yet they continue to admire beauty in everyday objects and to seek harmony with nature. Art is a part of daily life in Japan, and the culture is still shaped by the seasons. Kimono patterns, ink drawings on scrolls, and menus at home and in restaurants change according to the calendar.

Japanese meals are prepared to please the eye as well as the palate. Colors and shapes of vegetables, pickles, and fish or meat should, like nature itself, express harmony and beauty. Carrots often appear on one's plate cut in the shape of maple leaves. Come spring, rice cakes are tinted pink with azuki beans and wrapped in cherry leaves. Dishes set out for each meal also vary in shape, size, and color. In the United States, meals are generally served in courses, with the main serving heaped upon the plate, while in Japan, everything arrives at the same time in bite-sized pieces. Sweet, sour, salty, spicy, and bland are served at the same time, to be eaten alternately, since one taste is meant to complement another in a balance of flavors.

No meal is complete without *gohan,* or rice. Indeed, the Japanese words for breakfast, lunch, and dinner literally translate to "morning rice, "noon rice," and "evening rice." This staple is so important in Japanese culture that it was once used to determine a man's wealth and exchanged like money. Samurai were paid in rice, and the rank of a shogun was measured by the amount of rice he had. Throughout Japan, one still sees Shinto shrines dedicated to Inari, the rice god. *Tsukemono,* or pickles, usually end each meal, as they are considered an aid to digestion. There are supposedly over 4,000 varieties of Japanese pickles. They can be sweet, sour, or curried, and they are not always pickled in vinegar. The daikon, a long white radish, is the most popular pickle.

Lacquered, porcelain, and bamboo dishes filled with an amazing variety of tastes are brought to a low table, around which the guests sit upon cushions. Before picking up their chopsticks, they lift the scented *oshibori* from its bamboo basket to wipe their hands and face. This damp washcloth comes heated in winter and iced for summer. *"Itadakimasu,"* or "I receive," one says, taking up chopsticks and lifting the first bowl up to the mouth to scoop in the food. Meals begin and end with *ocha,* or green tea, which is also regularly served between meals, at school, and during breaks at work. Though the Japanese prefer their desserts *before* dinner, they will occasionally finish a meal with mandarin oranges, strawberries in season, or sweet bean or green tea ice cream. *Gochisosama-deshita,* or "Everything was delicious!"

JAPAN CRAFTS
Cool Secrets for Creating Great Crafts

- Read through the instructions—all the way—before you start. This tip can be hard to follow, because you might be so eager to start, you'll dive right in. That's the right spirit! But read all the way through anyway. You'll be glad you did.
- Gather all your materials first. A missing item might make you stop halfway through, and then you won't feel like finishing.
- Protect your work surface. Lay down newspaper or a plastic tablecloth. (This is a step your parents will be glad you took!) Wear old clothes.
- Be creative. You might think of a great new step to add or a twist that gives the craft your personal touch. While you're at it, learn from your mistakes. Try a craft a few times to get it right. Your craft doesn't have to look like the one in the picture to be great.
- Be careful. When the instructions tell you to get help from an adult, you know what you should do? You guessed it. *Get help from an adult!*
- Clean up right away. It's much easier to clean paintbrushes, wipe down surfaces, and wash tools (including your hands) while the mess is fresh. Plus, when you ask for permission to start a new project, you can remind your parents that you cleaned up last time. You could also ask your parents to join you. Crafts are even *more* fun when someone does them with you.
- As you go about your everyday activities, save things that might be good for your projects. Shoeboxes, toilet paper rolls, ribbon and tissue paper from a gift—these can all be used to make crafts that you'll enjoy keeping or giving to friends and family.
- The final secret? Have fun! If you don't enjoy it, there's no point in crafting.

Oshogatsu, or New Year's, is Japan's most important holiday. Families gather and businesses close for seasonal celebrations, usually from a few days before December 31 through January 4. All debts and household bills must be paid before the old year ends. Houses and offices are thoroughly cleaned and everything put in proper order. Ropes made of rice straw are traditionally hung by doorways with pine branches and bamboo stalks, while *kagami mochi,* rice cakes topped with a mandarin orange, including stem and leaf, are placed in entryways, all to honor ancient Shinto gods and ward off evil. New Year's greeting cards are mailed, and families and friends visit and exchange gifts. Children usually receive envelopes of money. Noodle shops stay open late on New Year's Eve because it is traditional to eat *toshi-koshi soba,* or year-bridging noodles, since they symbolize long life. To slurp noodles from a bowl held up to one's mouth is not considered rude, and one can hear a restaurant whose specialty is noodles long before arriving. Come midnight, the bells of all the temples in Japan toll 108 times. According to the Buddhist religion, 108 is the number of vices tempting humans, but these can be driven out by the clanging bells. The first dream of the New Year is considered significant as it predicts whatever fortune or failure is ahead. Families also traditionally visit shrines and temples.

Tips for the Kitchen

- Read through the recipe—*all the way*—before you start. Stopping halfway through the cooking process because you don't have the right ingredients or cookware is a waste of food. Plus, you'll still be hungry!
- Wear an apron. Wash your hands with warm water and soap before you start.
- Be very careful! Always get help from **an adult** when you are using the oven, the stovetop, or sharp knives. Use oven mitts to lift hot baking sheets and pans. Protect the counter with a trivet before you set down a hot container.
- Clean up right away. The sooner you do it, the easier it will be.
- Once you've made a recipe successfully, you can experiment the next time. Change the ingredients. Use blueberries instead of raspberries, or honey instead of sugar.
- Finally, share you food with your friends and family. Seeing people enjoy your cooking is as much fun as enjoying it yourself!

New Year's Parade

Ozoni

The Japanese welcome the first day of the New Year with a bowl of *ozoni*. Although the soup's vegetables and fish or fowl vary among families and from region to region, this seasonal soup must contain *mochi,* or sticky rice cakes, traditional symbols of wealth and purity. During New Year's, sumo wrestlers and other pop stars are featured on television and in the press, pounding barrels of hot steamed rice with huge mallets to make *mochi*. These are usually formed into round cakes symbolizing mirrors, one of the three sacred treasures of the Shinto gods (the others are a sword and jewel). *Mochi* is softened by dipping it in boiling water, then toasted and eaten with seasoned seaweed and soy sauce.

Preparation Time: 30 minutes
Cooking Time: 20 minutes

Ingredients:

5   dried shitake mushrooms
2   teaspoons sugar
2   cups chicken broth
2   carrots, peeled and sliced thin
8   medium shrimp (*ozoni* may be prepared with chicken or other seafood, but shrimp is particularly popular as its bent back honors old age and long life)
3   scallions
1   cup fresh pea pods
15 napa or Chinese cabbage leaves, chopped
    Several handfuls of fresh spinach, washed
1   tablespoon Japanese soy sauce
6   *mochi* rice cakes (available at Asian or health food stores)

Ozoni

1. Rinse mushrooms and soak them in 1½ cups water with ½ teaspoon sugar for about 15 minutes, until softened. Remove and squeeze them over their water. Save the water. Cut stems from mushrooms and discard. Chop the tops.
2. Add mushroom water to chicken broth and simmer with mushrooms and carrots 15 minutes.
3. Meanwhile, clean the shrimp. Drop them into boiling water in another saucepan for 3 minutes. Remove from stove, drain, and set aside.
4. Steam scallions, pea pods, napa leaves, and spinach, adding 1 tablespoon of soy sauce and the remaining sugar.
5. As soup slowly simmers, slice *mochi* into small squares and place them on a baking sheet an inch or more apart. Broil them 5 to 8 minutes at 400°F, turning them over once, until they are brown and puffy.
6. Ladle hot soup and vegetables in individual bowls, adding several *mochi* and shrimp on top.

Dashi

Dashi is broth made from fish stock and is the basis of many Japanese recipes. Instant dashi, premade and packaged into single small bags, is available at Asian markets. Although best used right away, dashi can be cooled, then covered and refrigerated for several days.

Preparation Time: Soak kombu overnight + 15 minutes
Cooking Time: 15 minutes

Ingredients:

6   cups cold water
    3-inch-square piece of kombu (dried kelp, also spelled *konbu*),
    washed and soaked in water overnight in the refrigerator.
1   cup *katsuobushi* flakes (bonito flakes, or dried, shaved tuna,
    usually found in Asian markets and health food stores)
2   teaspoons sugar
1/3 cup soy sauce

1. Pour cold water in saucepan and boil. Drain then rinse kombu and drop it in the pan until the water begins to boil again. Using tongs, remove kombu from the pan immediately (or it will cause the water to become bitter).
2. Stir bonito flakes into boiling water and turn off the burner.
3. Let the broth stand several minutes, until the *katsuobushi* goes to the bottom of the pan. Set a sieve over a bowl, and drain the broth through the sieve. Squeeze bonito flakes into the broth; discard the flakes.
4. Add sugar and soy sauce to the broth and stir.

Wish on a Daruma

Okiagari koboshi, or tumbler dolls, are sold almost everywhere during the New Year. Made of papier-mâché and usually painted bright red with black features and gold trim, they come in all sizes, yet never have arms, legs, or eyes. Most are weighted at the bottom, so when they are pushed over, they pop right back up. Japanese say, *"Nana korobi ya oki,"* or "Seven times rolling, eight times stand up," which means, "Keep trying no matter how hard something is and you will eventually succeed." Daruma dolls are good-luck symbols. One buys them blind and paints in one eye after making a wish. When that wish comes true, the owner rewards *Daruma* with its other eye. Politicians are often featured in the media painting in second eyes after winning elections. Businessmen display *Daruma* dolls in hopes of financial success. At the end of the year, it is customary to take one's *Daruma* to a temple and toss it into a bonfire, for once it has earned both eyes, it has served its purpose.

Daruma dolls were inspired by Bodhidharma, the priest who is considered the father of Zen Buddhism in Japan. This sect emphasizes meditation and withdrawal from the worries of this world. Bodhidharma meditated in the lotus position for nine years—such a long time that his arms and legs withered away.

Make a Daruma Doll

Your papier-mâche doll can be as small as an egg or bigger than a basketball.

You'll Need:

A round balloon
Newspapers and blank newsprint
A flat pan for the papier-mâche mix
White flour (or white glue)
Warm water
Bowl
Scissors
Pebbles
Paintbrushes
Acrylic or poster paints (traditionally red, black, white, gold)
Pencil

1. Blow up a round balloon and tie it.
2. Ripping from the fold down, tear old newspapers and blank newsprint into strips about 4 inches long and 1½ inches wide.
3. Slowly stir ½ cup of flour into ½ cup of warm water (or mix ½ cup of white glue with ½ cup of water). The solution should have the thickness of heavy cream. Add more water if it seems too thick.
4. Pull strips of newspaper through the solution one piece at a time. Hold each piece up to drain off any excess, pulling it gently between your fingers before adding it onto the form.
5. Place each strip over the one below in the opposite direction—one vertically, the next horizontally—until the balloon is covered with 5 or 6 layers. (Leave a hole at the bottom so that you can add small pebbles later for weight.) Alternate wet layers with strips of dry newspaper. Rolling several sheets of newsprint and covering them with the solution will give the doll more dimension. Use plain newsprint for the final layer.

6. Set the project on top of a bowl to dry for 24 hours or more, turning it several times so that it dries evenly.
7. When it is completely dry, pierce the balloon with scissors and remove it. Put pebbles in the bottom, then cover this opening with another few layers of papier-mâche.
8. Using scissors, carefully trim any loose pieces of newspaper, making the surface of the project as smooth as possible.
9. Paint the body a solid color (bright red is most common). Sketch out facial features with a pencil, then paint them with a fine brush. Draw circles for eyes, making sure they remain white and without pupils.
10. Add one pupil when you make a wish. Add the other pupil when your wish comes true.

Sukiyaki

Sukiyaki (pronounced *skee-YAH-kee*) is one of Japan's most popular *nabemono,* or one-pot, winter meals. It is usually cooked on the table, so diners can help themselves right from the simmering pot. As the juices from the vegetables and sauce mix with the meat, the taste gets better and better. *Sukiyaki* means "hoe-broiled." It got its name from farmers and samurai who, after hunting wild game, cooked their catch on shovels over open fires. These days, it's cooked in an electric frying pan or wok. The beef should be almost paper-thin, so ask the butcher to carve it on his machine.

In Japan, each guest is served a raw egg in a bowl. He or she then beats the egg and drags each piping hot morsel through it, coating all the vegetables and beef. Sukiyaki is ideal for any large gathering of family and friends.

Preparation Time: 20 minutes
Cooking Time: As long as guests are at the table

Ingredients:

1   pound beef tenderloin or chuck fillets, sliced very thin
1   teaspoon sesame oil
10 scallions
1   can drained bamboo shoots
½   head napa cabbage (or bok choy), cut into quarters
4   stalks celery
½   pound broccoli
2   medium carrots, peeled and sliced
½   pound fresh spinach
15–20 sugar snap pea pods
8   fresh mushrooms, sliced
14 ounces firm tofu, cut into one-inch cubes

For the sauce:
¾ cup Japanese soy sauce
4   teaspoons sugar
½ cup water
¼ cup dashi (or ½ cup chicken broth)

1. Cut all vegetables into bite-sized pieces. Arrange them and
   the tofu on a large platter and place it on the table.
2. Mix soy sauce, sugar, and water with dashi or chicken broth
   to make the sauce.
3. **Ask an adult** to grease the electric skillet or wok with the
   sesame oil.
4. Start by putting in a few slices of beef and pouring an inch of
   sauce into the pan. Have a pitcher of the sauce nearby to
   keep adding to the wok.
5. Add the different vegetables, the meat, and sauce alternately.
6. As the sukiyaki cooks, invite guests to help themselves from
   the simmering pan upon the table.

A *Sumi-e* for the Family *Tokonoma*

Japanese students are expected to learn at least a thousand Kanji ideograms in elementary school, and at New Year's they have the chance to show off their best writing skills through *sumi-e*. Each year during New Year's, the emperor sponsors a writing contest. A theme is announced and children all over Japan compete at painting poems using *sumi* ink. Winners are invited to read and exhibit at court. Some Japanese create calligraphy for scrolls to hang above seasonal flower arrangements in the *tokonoma,* or alcove at the main entrance to their home.

Brush painting is believed to improve one's character because it requires self-discipline and focus. *Sumi-e,* which means "Chinese black ink," is not just the art of painting letters—it must also capture the meaning behind the letters. A pine tree symbolizes long life, while a bamboo stalk stands for strength. Shades of black and gray invite one's imagination to complete scenes suggested by nature.

You'll Need

Newsprint or drawing paper for practice
Pencil
White cardboard or a sheet of white drawing paper or *shoji,*
    "rice paper," approximately 8 by 11 inches
Black and red tempura paint or *sumi* ink
Paintbrushes of several sizes, including #10
Several small dishes filled with water
Glue
A long sheet of colored paper such as wallpaper, approximately
    8 feet long and 3 feet wide—about the same size as the
    doorway over which it will hang
Two dowels approximately 4 feet long (precut dowels of various
    lengths are readily found at crafts supply stores)
Rounded screws (cup hooks) or picture hooks

1. Sketch out a design first in pencil. Keep it simple, since *sumi-e* is a mere suggestion of reality. Most subjects are inspired by nature.
2. Dilute the paint with water now and then. Dip the brush into the paint or ink lightly, using a small amount of paint at a time.
3. Start the drawing from the bottom of the paper, working upward and allowing the paint to become thinner as the lines move up. Try to keep moving the brush without stopping the flow of paint. Draw with large strokes, starting with jet-black, then adding more water for shades of gray. Finish it off with a few red highlights.
4. To make a scroll, cut the long sheet of colored paper or wallpaper to be two inches wider than your picture on each side. Brush a line of glue across each end of the scroll, and roll the bottom and top onto the dowels.
5. Glue your *sumi* painting in the middle of the scroll, then hang it using rounded screws or picture hooks.

Kokeshi Dolls

It is believed that *kokeshi*—simple wooden dolls—originated in northeastern Japan more than 300 years ago, during the Tokugawa period, where they were sold as keepsakes to travelers who went to Tohoku for that region's healing hot springs. People living in rural areas came to associate *kokeshi* with a bountiful harvest and encouraged their children to play with them in order to please the gods.

The cherry, maple, or dogwood from which the dolls are fashioned is left outside to season from one to five years. Artisans make *kokeshi* dolls on lathes, and they range in size from two inches to over two feet tall. The unique handcrafted creations have circular, painted heads atop colorful bodies but no limbs. Their hair, eyes, and eyebrows are represented by mere lines, with facial expressions varying from smiling to serious or sad. *Kokeshi* dolls are treasured for their simplicity, and because they are traditionally handmade, no two are the same. These dolls are classic examples of Japanese folk art.

Create a *Kokeshi*

You'll Need

Glue
Brush for spreading glue
Sheets of origami paper with
    colorful designs
Cardboard tube from toilet paper
    roll
Scissors
Ping-Pong ball
Black and red markers with fine tips

1. Using glue and a brush, paste a colorful sheet of origami paper around an empty toilet paper tube for the doll's kimono. If the origami sheets are too small to fit completely around the roll, cut and paste another strip to fit down the back.
2. Draw facial features and hair on a Ping-Pong ball with fine markers. Use fine black lines for eyes and thin red lines for lips to make your *kokeshi* doll look more traditional.
3. Glue the Ping-Pong ball head to the top of the cardboard roll or inside the doll's kimono collar.
4. Cut two horizontal sheets about ½ inch each from a different origami pattern. Glue one piece around the doll's neck to form a high collar for the kimono. Glue the other strip around the waist to make an obi, or sash.

Miso Soup

It's soup for breakfast in Japan! And it's usually the same soup served at the start of most meals, whether at home or at a restaurant. Miso is also used in salad dressings and sauces. Made from fermented soybeans, barley, or brown rice, miso is quite salty. It comes in white or red varieties, depending on specific ingredients, and is usually found in the refrigerated section of health food stores. Like Grandmother's chicken soup, miso provides quick energy and is a cure-all for complaints from head colds to upset stomachs.

Preparation Time: 5
Cooking Time: 10 minutes

Ingredients:

2   cups water
½ cup dashi
2   tablespoons miso paste
¼ pound of tofu, cut into half inch pieces
3   small rectangles of nori (seaweed, called *laver* in English)
1   scallion, sliced thin

1. Boil water and dashi.
2. Stir miso paste into hot broth until dissolved. Do not let it boil. Add tofu.
3. Ladle miso into individual bowls. Garnish with nori and scallions.

Teriyaki Salmon

Because it is a nation of islands, the Japanese have always looked to the sea to provide much of their food. They used to eat whale meat regularly, but since this mammal is now endangered, most have given it up due to environmental awareness and increasing political criticism.

Salmon, especially eaten raw as sushi, is especially popular among the Japanese, although nowadays much of it is imported from Alaska. They also enjoy octopus and squid, raw or cooked, as well as *unagi,* or eel. A favorite snack of Japanese children is sweet dried squid.

Preparation Time: 4 hours
Cooking Time: 15 minutes

Ingredients:

2	tablespoons sesame oil
4	tablespoons soy sauce
2	tablespoons brown sugar
1	teaspoon ginger root, peeled and grated juice of 2 fresh lemons
½	onion, diced
2	cloves garlic, pressed
1	pound wild salmon fillets (about 4 pieces)

1. Mix 1 tablespoon of sesame oil, soy sauce, brown sugar, ginger, lemon juice, onion, and garlic to make the teriyaki sauce. Refrigerate.
2. Cut salmon into individual portions and add it to the sauce. Refrigerate three hours or more, turning it several times
3. Remove salmon from teriyaki sauce. Set sauce aside for later.
4. Put 1 tablespoon sesame oil in a shallow baking dish, and brush salmon with sesame oil on both sides.
5. **Ask an adult** to help you broil salmon 6 minutes on each side.
6. When salmon is cooked through, pour the teriyaki sauce over it, turning the fish several times to coat it evenly.

Edamame

Teriyaki salmon served with boiled rice and edamame makes a satisfying meal. These soybeans are boiled or steamed in their pods, then salted. Edamame is often served as an appetizer in Japanese restaurants and is a popular snack between meals. Pull each piece between your teeth to release the fat beans, then discard the fuzzy pod. They are yummy hot or cold.

Cooking Time: About 10 minutes

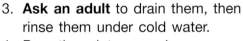

Ingredients:

1   pound package of frozen edamame
2   tablespoons soy sauce
1   tablespoon butter

1. Fill a pan with 6 cups of water and **ask an adult** to bring it to a boil. Carefully add the frozen edamame to the boiling water.
2. When the water returns to a boil, cook 5 more minutes or until beans are tender but still firm.
3. **Ask an adult** to drain them, then rinse them under cold water.
4. Pour them into a serving bowl. Add soy sauce and butter, and stir.

Fly a Carp for Courage— Children's Day

Fish fly outside houses and from apartment balconies all over Japan on the fifth of May. *Koi-nobori,* colorful windsocks in the shape of carp, swim in the breeze to celebrate Kodomo no Hi, or Children's Day. The largest fish is placed at the top of a tall bamboo pole, honoring the eldest child. Fluttering in the wind, they seem to swim just as carp do, against swift currents and waterfalls. The koi's courage and determination against life's difficulties are qualities that Japanese parents wish to see in their children. Usually flown for several days, *koi-nobori,* like flags, are taken down each evening. Otherwise, their colors might bleed and fade in the rain.

It is also the season to change flower arrangements to irises in the *tokonoma,* as well as changing the household scroll. The iris, with petals resembling ancient swords, symbolizes strength and courage.

Japanese boys and girls used to be celebrated on different days with different customs, but since Japan embraced democracy, both genders share the traditional Boys' Day. However, *hina-matsuri,* the festival for girls, continues to be honored by most families on the third day of the third month. Dolls, dressed in beautiful brocaded robes to represent members of the ancient imperial court, have been passed down through generations. These family treasures are set up on tiers and displayed one day each year. Daughters invite friends in to share pink-and-white rice dumplings with plum wine beside vases of peach blossoms, which symbolize gentle female qualities and happiness in marriage.

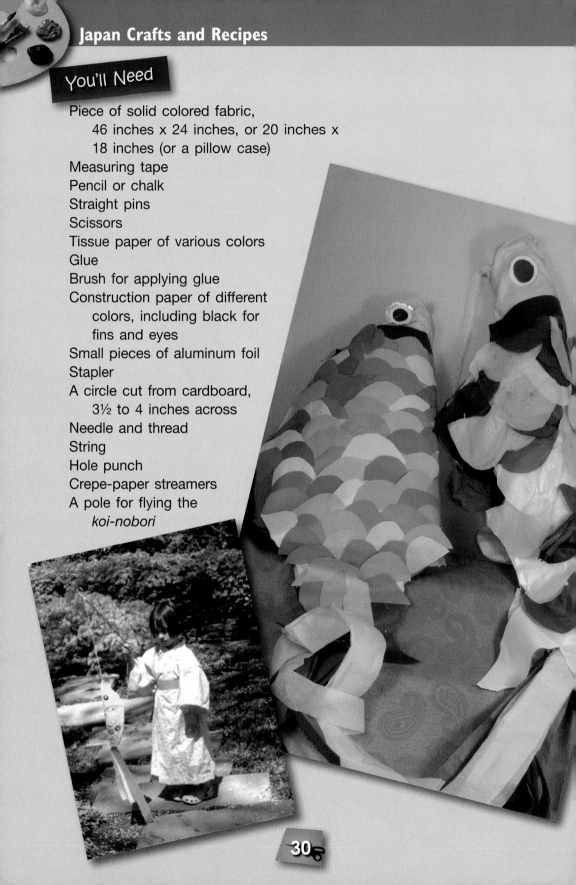

You'll Need

Piece of solid colored fabric,
    46 inches x 24 inches, or 20 inches x
    18 inches (or a pillow case)
Measuring tape
Pencil or chalk
Straight pins
Scissors
Tissue paper of various colors
Glue
Brush for applying glue
Construction paper of different
    colors, including black for
    fins and eyes
Small pieces of aluminum foil
Stapler
A circle cut from cardboard,
    3½ to 4 inches across
Needle and thread
String
Hole punch
Crepe-paper streamers
A pole for flying the
    koi-nobori

1. Fold fabric in half lengthwise. Using chalk or pencil, sketch the outline of a fish so that the belly is on the fold of the cloth. Pin the sides together to keep the cloth from slipping and cut out the fish, stopping 4 inches from the front.
2. Cut out lots of different-colored 3-inch half-circles from tissue paper and/or construction paper to make rows of fish scales. Fold them like fans.
3. Open the fabric, and using a minimum amount of glue, lay scales across the fish's body, overlapping one row at a time all the way to the fish's tail.
4. Cut out fins from black construction paper. Paste or staple these to the top and bottom of the fish's body.
5. Cut out two large eyes from black construction paper and two larger circles of aluminum foil. Place each black circle over a silver one, then glue or staple these on each side of the head.
6. To add dimension, cut a strip of black construction paper 1 inch wide and glue this behind the eyes along the front of the start of the scales.
7. Cut out a cardboard strip about 1 inch wide, long enough to go around the inside of the fish's mouth. Fold the fabric at the mouth around this ring. Secure it all the way around with pins. With a needle and thread, sew the cardboard circle into the fabric.
8. Sew the two long sides of the fish together. Stop about 3 inches before reaching the mouth and the tail, so they remain open to allow the wind to blow through.
9. Cut a piece of string 20 inches long. Using the hole punch, make two holes through the fabric and cardboard ring, on opposite sides of the mouth. Tie the string to the holes.
10. Cut different-colored crepe paper streamers, 2 or 3 feet long, and attach these to the tail.
11. Tie a longer string to the first one and raise your carp on a pole to catch the breeze.

Yakitori

Summer in Japan begins after the rainy season, and with it comes the feeling known as *assari,* a more laid-back lifestyle. Pictures in the *tokonoma* are changed to summer flowers, butterflies, or fish jumping waterfalls. Everyone seems to be enjoying cold buckwheat noodles served over ice cubes, and the air is filled with the smell of yakitori, marinated shish kebabs, being barbecued over charcoal fires at street stalls.

If you use wooden skewers to make your kebabs, be sure to soak them for a half hour before threading on the food. This will keep the skewers from burning while the yakitori cooks.

Preparation Time: 10 minutes; marinate 8 hours; then 10 more minutes
to thread skewers
Cooking Time: 8 minutes

Ingredients:

2   chicken breasts, skinned and boned
1/3 cup Japanese soy sauce
2   tablespoons sugar
1½ tablespoons fresh lemon juice
½   teaspoon fresh ginger root, finely grated
1   garlic clove, finely grated
1   teaspoon grated daikon (white radish) or white turnip
2   bunches of scallions with green tops and roots removed
¼   cup sesame oil

1. Cut chicken into bite-sized chunks. Mix soy sauce, sugar, lemon juice, grated ginger, garlic, and daikon to make a sauce.
2. Add chicken. Cover and marinate in refrigerator overnight.
3. Remove chicken from sauce and arrange alternately on skewers with scallions.

4. **Ask an adult** to boil the marinade, then let it cool.
5. Add sesame oil to the marinade, then brush it on the skewered chicken and scallions.
6. **Ask an adult** to broil the kebabs on a grill five minutes on each side or in oven at least 3 inches below broiler (so as not to burn the wooden skewers).
7. Pour remaining sauce over them, then serve.

Simple but Useful Fans

Yukatas, or cool cotton kimonos, are worn in summer, and everyone seems to be carrying a fan. In Japanese culture, fans represent much more than a way to keep cool. Novels and poetry written centuries ago, as well as historical and modern Japanese theater productions, include an entire language of gestures that use fans to express emotions.

You can buy decorative paper for this project, or you can use plain paper and decorate it with scenes from nature.

You'll Need:

Heavy decorative paper 12 inches x 12 inches (as used for
    scrapbooking); or decorate your own paper
Masking tape
Scissors
Stapler
Pieces of ribbon about a foot long

1. Place paper on a flat surface and fold it horizontally 1 inch from the bottom. Turn the paper over and firmly crease it inch by inch, first one side, then the other, making accordion pleats to the end of the paper.
2. Twist the fan 1½ inches from the bottom and staple it to form a handle.
3. Wind masking tape around this stem and tie ribbon around the tape to cover it. Let the ends of the ribbon dangle.

Obon Festival
Make a Paper Lantern

Obon, the Buddhist Festival of the Dead, is celebrated throughout Asia and has been observed in Japan ever since Buddhism arrived from India by way of China, 1,300 years ago. The religious festival is observed from July 13 through 15 or from August 13 through 16, depending on whether the lunar or solar calendar is followed. By visiting temples and family graves, Japanese honor their ancestors, whose spirits are believed to return to earth at this time. Some honor the old traditions by burning incense at gravesites and setting out rice cakes to welcome back the departed, then lead them back to their former homes with lanterns, where foods and the friends they most loved on earth await. Buddhist priests are invited to chant sutras, or special prayers for the dead.

On the final night of the festival, tiny boats, usually made of reeds and straw, are set adrift in streams or calm waters. Floating paper lanterns, called *toro nagashi,* are lighted and placed in the bow, while scented incense sticks smoke from the stern. The boats often carry personal messages to the dead. Many believe these lanterns ward off evil spirits. *Bon-odori* dances are performed while fireworks help guide the dead back to their final resting place.

The shapes of Japanese paper lanterns vary from circles and squares to bells and animal figures. If you have a pool or pond in your backyard, you can make a bunch and float them at a family outdoor party.

**Never leave lighted candles unattended, and
never allow the flame to touch the paper.**

Fine point, permanent black marker
4 sheets rice paper or YUPO™ translucent paper, 8 inches x 12 inches
    or 9 inches x 17 inches
Bamboo skewers (4 per lantern)
Styrofoam block about one foot square and one inch thick (or a clean
    rectangular Styrofoam tray such as a meat tray)
Transparent tape
Glue

Paintbrush

Paper clips

Toothpicks

Tea candle and matches (optional)

Tissue paper (optional)

1. Using a permanent marker, sketch trees, flowers, or other natural
   scenes on all four sheets of rice paper. You might also write a
   short message to someone who has died.
2. Carefully push a skewer into each corner of the Styrofoam base,
   about half an inch down, to form the walls of your frame. Be sure
   to leave plenty of room at the edges so that the lantern won't tip
   over and into the water under a gentle breeze.
3. When your drawing is dry, wrap the sides of each piece of paper
   around a skewer, and secure it by brushing on glue. Use paper
   clips to hold the paper and bamboo skewers tightly together while
   the glue dries.
4. Stick a toothpick halfway down into the Styrofoam base. Then
   gently push the bottom of a small candle onto the other half of the
   toothpick to hold it secure.
5. **With adult assistance,** light a small candle and place it in the
   lantern. After dark, set your lantern afloat in a gentle breeze.

Snack Foods
Cucumber Sushi Rolls

Obentos, or honorable lunchboxes, are traditionally square or rectangular, with two or three tiers, and made of lacquered wood or plastic. Japanese fill these boxes with fried sweet tofu pockets filled with rice. These are eaten with slices of sweet pickled ginger or *onigiri,* which is as popular with Japanese children as peanut butter and jelly sandwiches are for American kids. *Onigiri* are rice balls wrapped in nori, or dried seaweed, usually with seafood or pickled plums in the middle. The bento box is then placed in a *furoshiki,* which is a large silk scarf knotted at opposite ends to make a bag suitable for carrying on picnics, to school, or to sporting events. *Ekiben* is the nickname for "station lunch." Bought at train stops, each is crammed full of small portions of food typical of the region near the station.

Cucumber Sushi Rolls

Sushi does not always mean "raw fish" in Japan. This vegetarian snack is called *kappa maki,* after Kappa, the legendary River-Boy, a troublemaker of Japanese folklore who dwells in streams and rivers. His body resembles that of a tortoise, though he has frog's legs and a monkey-like head that is hollow on top to hold his power. In earlier times, Kappa was blamed for every drowning. Because he was particularly fond of cucumbers, mothers protected their children by tossing cucumbers into the water before allowing them to go swimming.

Since Japanese usually cut their cucumbers lengthwise, English or European cucumbers, which have smaller seeds, work best in this recipe. They are accompanied by slices of sweet pickled ginger. Crabmeat, *kanpyo* (dried gourd strips), salmon, and slices of sweet omelet are also popular choices in sushi rolls.

When making sushi, a bamboo mat is helpful for making your roll even and tight. If you don't have one, you can use aluminum foil instead.

Preparation Time: 45 minutes
Cooking Time: 20 minutes
(rice)

Ingredients:

1   cup sushi-style rice
     to 2 cups water
1½ tablespoons sugar
2   English or European cucumbers
2   raw carrots
1   tablespoon rice vinegar
3   tablespoons water
2   large sheets of dried nori (laver in English)
     sweet ginger, sliced
     soy sauce

1. Cook the rice according to package directions and let it cool. Add the sugar.
2. **Under adult supervision,** peel cucumbers and carrots; cut them into thin strips 4 inches long.
3. Mix rice vinegar with water.
4. Place one nori sheet, shiny side down, on a bamboo mat. Moisten your hands with the vinegar-and-water mixture and spread rice evenly, ¼ inch thick, over nori sheet, leaving an inch at each end.
5. Lay several slices of cucumbers and carrots on the rice.
6. Carefully roll up the bamboo mat.
7. Unroll the mat gently and allow the roll to sit 5 minutes or more.
8. **Under adult supervision,** carefully cut the roll into 2-inch-long pieces.
9. Serve with slices of sweet ginger and bowls of soy sauce for dipping.

Kitsune Tofu

According to Japanese folklore, the *kitsune,* or fox, is crazy about fried tofu, or bean curd. Tofu can be boiled, fried, barbecued, baked, dried, or eaten raw. It is very good for one's health and amazingly versatile, since it takes on the flavor of whatever is cooked with it. It will keep more than a week in the refrigerator, but only if the fresh water in which it sits is changed daily.

Preparation Time: 8 hours to marinate
Cooking Time: 20 minutes

Ingredients:

1   pound extra-firm tofu
⅓   cup dashi
1½ tablespoons soy sauce
1   tablespoon sugar
2   tablespoons sesame oil
     Grated fresh ginger
     Grated daikon (white radish)

1. Drain tofu and press as dry as possible between paper towels. Cut it into 10 slices, each a quarter inch wide. Lay them out in a baking dish.
2. Mix dashi, soy sauce, and sugar and pour it over the tofu. Cover and marinate in refrigerator overnight.
3. Drain the tofu, setting the sauce aside for later.
4. **Under adult supervision,** heat a skillet with sesame oil on medium heat. Add tofu slices.
5. Press slices gently with spatula until they sizzle. Turn slices and do the same on the other side. Brush each piece of tofu with soy sauce mixture on both sides as it cooks.
6. Place tofu slices on paper towels to drain.
7. Garnish with fresh ginger slices and grated fresh daikon. Serve with the reserved sauce for dipping.

Kitsune mask to celebrate Fox Night Festival

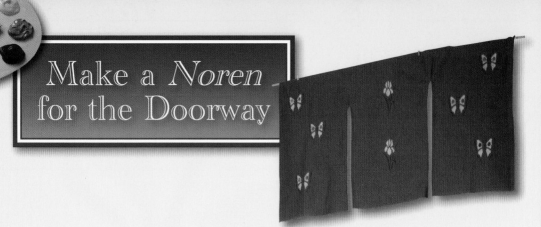

Make a *Noren* for the Doorway

Summer breezes in Japan bring the sound of tinkling wind chimes and the sight of *noren* flapping in the doorways of shops and restaurants. These decorative short curtains are slit from the bottom into two or three separate parts. They also serve as room dividers in Japanese homes and inns. *Noren* come in a variety of colors, and are usually silk-screened or stenciled with business logos, family crests, or designs from nature.

You'll Need:

3 yards of solid-colored cotton or muslin cloth, 36 inches wide (not too dark, as stenciled colors should show clearly)
Measuring tape
White chalk
Scissors or pinking shears for cutting fabric
Straight pins
Sewing needle
Thread same color as fabric
Several sheets of plain newsprint
Masking tape
An assortment of precut plastic stencils (available at craft stores)
Stencil brushes (with flat, rather than pointed, ends)
Fabric paints
Paper towels
Iron and ironing board
A dowel or curtain rod ½ inch in diameter
Hooked screws

1. Measure the width of the doorway where you plan to hang your *noren*.
2. Lay the cloth out on a long table and fold it into three equal parts. Using the measuring tape and chalk, mark the folds and mark where the stenciled designs will go.
3. Cut the fabric ⅔ up along the marked lines, leaving one inch on each side of all three pieces. Leave 2 inches at the top of each piece for inserting the dowel.
4. Sew a ¼-inch hem along the bottom and sides of the three panels. Measure 1½ inches down from the top, anchor with straight pins, and hem.
5. Layer pieces of plain newsprint on your work table to protect it from the paint.
6. Lay one section of fabric at a time over the newsprint. Tape a stencil tightly onto the fabric to keep it from moving and to prevent any paint from seeping underneath.

7. Using a different stencil brush for each color, apply a small amount of fabric paint, working from the outside of the stencil toward the center of the design. Keep the brush as dry as possible to avoid any leaking or blotting. Dab your brush on a paper towel to remove any excess paint. Use the minimum amount of paint with a light, dotting touch of the brush rather than broad strokes. If you use the same stencil more than once, make sure it is clean and dry before you retape it.

8. When finished stenciling, place the fabric between sheets of newsprint on an ironing board. Set designs with a medium-hot iron.

9. Slide a dowel through the top hem. Screw in hooks over the doorway and hang up the *noren*.

Autumn Means Moon Viewing
Tsukimi Soba—
Moon-Viewing Noodles

The Japanese people's fondness for nature is evident in such customs as moon viewing. A special time is set aside to honor the harvest moon in mid-September or October, depending on the lunar calendar. When Japanese look up at the bright, full moon, they see a rabbit pounding *mochi*, not the Man in the Moon. A full moon is also a symbol of harmony and family unity.

A pyramid of sweet dumplings, or moon-shaped rice cakes, topped with a mandarin orange, its stem and leaf intact, is placed atop a low table in one's apartment terrace or veranda, in the light of the moon. This table usually stands next to an arrangement of autumn grasses and offerings of beans and seasonal chestnuts. The feathery plumes of the pampas plant, chrysanthemums, and other fall flowers are featured in the household *tokonoma*, and writing poems in calligraphy with autumn themes is encouraged. Families and friends often plan mountain hikes for the purpose of enjoying better views of the moon.

Originally a celebration of thanksgiving for annual rice harvests, many people are too busy with work and school these days to take time out to observe traditional customs. However, most Japanese do remember to eat a bowl of *tsukimi soba*, or moon-viewing noodles.

To Japanese, the yellow yolk of the egg against its white resembles the full harvest moon shining among clouds. If you don't like soft eggs, hard-boiled ones cut in half and served on top of the noodles will still symbolize the full moon.

Preparation Time: 15 minutes
Cooking Time: 20 minutes

One package soba
(buckwheat noodles)
1   tablespoon sesame oil
4   scallions
1   cup fresh mushrooms,
    sliced
½   cup sugar pea pods
1   cup dashi (or one chicken bouillon
    cube)
1½ cups chicken broth
1   tablespoon soy sauce
½   package or 5 ounces fresh baby spinach
1   fresh egg for each bowl

1. Boil soba according to package directions. Drain and set aside.
2. In a tablespoon of sesame oil, sauté chopped scallions with sliced
   mushrooms and sugar peas.
3. Heat chicken broth and dashi and soy sauce together in a soup
   pan.
4. To the hot broth, add cooked, drained noodles and spinach, along
   with the mushrooms, sugar peas, and scallions. Stir and cook for
   5 minutes.
5. Using a slotted spoon, dip noodles and vegetables out of broth
   and into soup bowls.
6. Break an egg over each helping. Have **an adult** quickly pour
   boiling soup over each egg, being very careful not to break the
   yolk. The boiling broth will immediately cook the egg.

A Beckoning Cat Brings Good Luck

The *Maneki Neko,* or Beckoning Cat, usually made of porcelain, is found in shops and homes throughout Japan. Merchants put this good-luck symbol, also known as Welcoming Cat or Money Cat, in the front windows of their stores and restaurants to draw people inside. The cat greets customers with its raised paw, usually the left one, which may even hold a coin to promise financial success. Nowadays, some are battery-powered with a moving paw facing outward, since Japanese extend invitations by waving hands toward a person, which means "bye-bye" in the West. *Maneki Neko* come in different colors, materials, and decor, though most are painted white with black spots and large yellow eyes. White represents purity, while black is supposed to ward off evil. In addition to the usual clay sculptures, Beckoning Cats can be toys, key chains, piggy banks—even decorations on sneakers.

According to Japanese folklore, the beckoning cat dates back to the seventeenth century and a Buddhist priest living in poverty in a Tokyo temple. Although he had little food, this kind priest shared whatever he had with his pet cat, Tama. One day, during a terrible storm, a wealthy samurai found shelter beneath the big tree near the temple. As the samurai waited for the storm to pass, he noticed the priest's cat beckoning him to come inside the temple. Just as the samurai left the tree to enter the temple, a bolt of lightning struck the tree. From that time on, the samurai, convinced the cat had saved his life, made sure that the priest and his beloved pet never went hungry again.

Sheet of plastic
3 pounds of clay (to make a cat about 6 inches tall)
Bowl of warm water
Craft sticks and other tools for sculpting clay
Tempera or acrylic paints: white, black, orange
Paintbrushes

1. Cover work area with a sheet of plastic.
2. Make a clay sphere the size of a tennis ball. Pinch features into this to create the cat's face.
3. Wet your fingers and roll two small clay balls and press them on top of the head. Pinch the cat's ears into points and continue shaping the original ball to make a realistic face for the cat.
4. Roll more clay to make a ball three times larger than the head.
5. Make three smaller balls, then roll each one into the shape of hot dogs to form back legs and a tail. Wet your fingers and press these firmly onto the body.
6. Roll the front legs in the same manner. Attach one paw so that it will sit on the floor, and extend the other paw in an upright position.
7. Smooth the cat all over with moist fingers.
8. Use a craft stick or clay tool to scratch in the cat's toes.
9. If your cat has trouble sitting up straight, insert a craft stick down into the body and up into the head. Keep all joints moistened, since clay shrinks as it dries.
10. Let the clay dry 24 hours or longer before painting it.

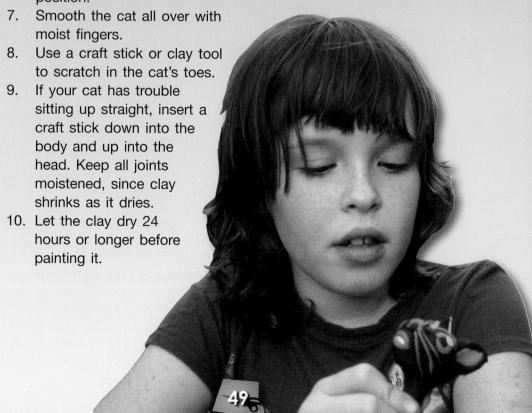

Chawan-Mushi

Chawan-mushi—a steamed custard appetizer—is a special favorite of Japanese children. It is common in late fall when ginkgo nuts are in season. The silvery nuts inside stinky ginkgo seeds are considered delicacies when roasted. The ginkgo tree, with its straight trunk, leaves shaped like small fans, and foul-smelling seeds, is native to China. Because it is known to have lived 250 million years ago, it has been called a living fossil. Its bad smell keeps the insects away, and it can withstand extreme weather conditions. Scientists believe the ginkgo is a link between ferns and flowering plants. They also believe it contains properties that improve memory function.

Preparation Time: 15 minutes
Cooking Time: 15-20 minutes

Ingredients:

1	cup dashi (or chicken broth)
1½	tablespoon soy sauce
1	chicken breast without skin, cut into ½-inch pieces
1	tablespoon sugar
4	eggs
¼	cup shaved raw carrots
3	fresh mushrooms, diced
	Several handfuls of fresh spinach, washed and chopped
½	cup snow peas
1	3-ounce can of *ginnan* (ginkgo nuts) or, if unavailable, water chestnuts, drained

1. Mix dashi or chicken broth with 1 tablespoon soy sauce in a pan. **Under adult supervision,** bring to a boil on the stove.
2. Add chicken, remaining soy sauce, and sugar to dashi. Simmer for 5 minutes.

3. Beat eggs lightly in a large bowl. Add shaved carrots, mushrooms, spinach, snow peas, and *ginnan* or water chestnuts, sliced thin.
4. Allow the broth to cool. Add egg mixture to the broth.
5. Ladle everything equally into 3 or 4 custard cups.
6. Cover the custard cups (use foil if they don't have lids) and place them in a bamboo steamer set over a pan of boiling water on top of the stove. Steam over medium heat about 15 to 20 minutes. Check to make sure that the pan remains half full of water. Add more water if needed. If you don't have a steamer, place custard cups in pan half-filled with hot water and bake in the oven at 350°F for 15 to 20 minutes.
7. *Chawan-mushi* is done when a toothpick or cake tester inserted in the center comes out clean.

Garden on a Tray

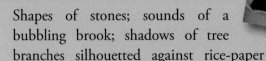

Shapes of stones; sounds of a bubbling brook; shadows of tree branches silhouetted against rice-paper windows—the Japanese admire and identify with nature.

Few live in houses with yards big enough to raise flower gardens, so they find ways of enjoying nature through art. They reshape trees and other living plants into tiny, gnarled bonsai in pots, and create miniature gardens of sand and stones on trays. The most famous life-sized garden in Japan is in Ryoanji, the Zen Buddhist Temple of the Peaceful Dragon, which is in Kyoto. This dry landscape inspires visitors to escape the stress of worldly worries through meditation. The arrangement created by raked sand and rocks supposedly symbolizes jagged mountains rising from the sea, like the country of Japan itself.

You can make a miniature garden on a tray, in a shallow box, or on a tabletop in the classroom.

You'll Need:

Pencil and paper
Modeling clay (if you wish to add hills to your landscape)
A tray with raised edges or a shallow box
A piece of cardboard or plastic sheet the same size as the tray or box
Glue
Brush for glue
2 pounds of fine sand (available at garden supply stores)
Stones of various shapes, sizes, textures, and colors
Rocks, twigs, small pieces of driftwood, or other found objects from
    nature
A small mirror (as from an old compact)
A wide-toothed comb, fork, or toothpick
Craft sticks to build a fence around your garden (optional)

Ryoanji, the Zen Buddhist Temple
of the Peaceful Dragon

1. Design your miniature Zen garden with pencil and paper. Decide if you wish to include a fence or a pond. Determine the pattern for the rocks.
2. Cover the bottom of the tray or box with a piece of cardboard or a plastic sheet. Mold several small hills out of clay, placing them on the tray according to your garden design.
3. On this, spread a thin layer of glue. Lightly sprinkle on the first layer of sand to cover the glue. If the sand is too coarse and pebbly, put it through a sifter.
4. Place any other items you want, such as stones, twigs, and a mirror.
5. Pour in another layer or so of sand. Using a comb, fork, or toothpick, carefully rake the sand around the items. Sprinkle water on the sand if it is too dry to rake.
6. Use craft sticks to build a fence around your garden, if you desire.

Katsu-domburi

Domburi (or *donburi*) meals are named for the "big bowls" in which they are served. This pork-and-veggie omelet over rice is Japanese "comfort food," and more common today in rural areas. Made with chicken, it's called *oyako domburi*, which means "mother and child."

Preparation Time: 20 minutes
Cooking Time: 40 minutes

Ingredients:

1	cup white rice
2	cups water
4	medium eggs
½	cup dashi
½	cup chicken broth
1	pound lean pork cutlet, sliced ⅛ inch thick
½	cup bread crumbs
2	tablespoons sesame oil
1	large onion, sliced thin
2	cups raw cabbage, sliced (as for slaw)
1	tablespoon soy sauce
1	tablespoon sugar
	sweet ginger, sliced

1. Cook 1 cup of rice in 2 cups water and set aside.
2. In a large bowl, beat eggs lightly. Add dashi and chicken broth.
3. Dip the pork in egg mixture and coat it with bread crumbs.
4. Sauté the pork in 1 tablespoon sesame oil for about 3 minutes on each side. Remove from the pan and set it aside.

5. Put the other tablespoon of sesame oil, onions, cabbage, soy sauce, and sugar into the pan and simmer on low while stirring. Put the pork back into the pan with the vegetables.

6. Add beaten eggs and broth, pouring it evenly over pork and veggies.

7. Cook on low heat, with the pan covered, 20 minutes or until the eggs are set. Turn the meat and omelet over once. Gently poke holes in the omelet to check that it is cooked through.

8. Spoon the cooked rice into *domburi* bowls and place the pork omelet on top. Serve with slices of sweet ginger.

Origami Paper Cranes

Folding paper has been a popular Japanese craft since the sixth century, when paper was first imported from China. Paper was so expensive that at first, only noblemen and ladies of the court were permitted to use it. Poems, love notes, and political secrets were frequently hidden in folded paper. Even the colors selected held secret messages. The first instructional manual on origami, *The Secret of One Thousand Cranes,* was published in 1797.

The crane is a bird of special beauty and grace, and because cranes mate for life, they symbolize loyalty for the Japanese. It is said that anyone who folds 1,000 paper cranes is guaranteed a long and happy life. It has become an international symbol of peace. Thus, origami cranes are common gifts at weddings and for new babies. Since origami teaches concentration and motor skills, most Japanese children learn this art in preschool or are taught at home by grandparents.

Origami paper, in a variety of solid colors or with kimono-like designs, is available in craft stores and bookstores, where one can also find instructional books for many different origami projects.

1. Starting best-side up, fold the square on the diagonal from one corner to the other.

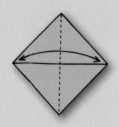

2. Unfold this, then fold on the opposite diagonal. Unfold and turn the square of paper over.

3. Fold the paper in half to make rectangles. Unfold it and fold it in half again the other way. Leave it folded this way.

4. Hold the paper so that the open edges point up. Bring the top corners together so that the paper bends on your diagonal creases.

5. Place the paper flat. There should be two flaps on each side. Place the paper so that the open corner is at the top and the closed corner is at the bottom. Fold the top flaps on the front to the middle so that the bottom edges meet in the middle.

6. Turn the paper over and do the same on the back. It should look like a small kite.

7. Now, fold the top triangle down and then up again. Turn your paper over and repeat. It should still be kite-shaped, but now it has an added horizontal crease.

8. Open the front flaps and lift the bottom corner up so that it folds again on the horizontal crease.

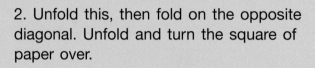

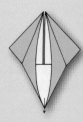

9. Pull one layer of the top corner all the way back. The edges will fold in on the side creases, making the paper diamond-shaped. Turn the paper over and do this same step on the other side.

10. Fold the bottom part of the flaps so that the outer edges touch the center of the paper. Turn your paper over and do the same thing on the other side.

11. Turn the two long points up, then fold the sides in to the center.

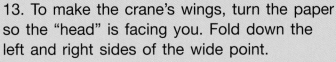

12. Decide which of the two points will be the head and fold that point down and crease it. Fold the "leg" backward on the folds just made.

13. To make the crane's wings, turn the paper so the "head" is facing you. Fold down the left and right sides of the wide point.

14. Gently blow into the hole at the bottom to inflate the crane's body. Tug on the wings so that the bird's body flattens.

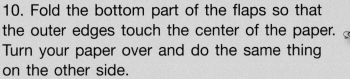

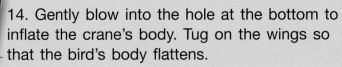

Further Reading

Books

Carnell, Kari. *Holiday Cooking Around the World.* Minneapolis: Lerner Publications, 2002.

Coerr, Eleanor. *Sadako and the 1000 Paper Cranes.* New York: Yearling, 1979 (Fiction).

Ishii, Takeyuki. *One Thousand Paper Cranes: The Story of Sadako and the Children's Peace Statue.* New York: Laurel Leaf, 2001.

McManus, Lori. *Meet Our New Student from Japan.* Hockessin, DE: Mitchell Lane Publishers, 2010.

Phillips, Charles. *Japan: Countries of the World.* Washington, DC: National Geographic, 2007.

Riccardi, Victoria Abbott. *Untangling My Chopsticks: A Culinary Sojourn in Kyoto.* New York: Random House, 2003.

Watanabe, Etsuko. *My Japan.* San Diego, CA: Kane/Miller Publishers, 2009.

Weston, Reiko. *Cooking the Japanese Way (Easy Menu Ethnic Cookbooks).* Minneapolis: Lerner Publishing Group, 2002.

Works Consulted

Andoh, Elizabeth. *Washoku: Recipes from the Japanese Home Kitchen.* Berkeley, CA & Toronto, Canada: Ten Speed Press, 2005.

Braman, Arlette N. *Kids Around the World Create! The Best Crafts & Activities from Many Lands.* Hoboken, NJ: John Wiley & Sons, 1999.

Dick Blick Art Materials: *"Japanese Floating Lanterns."* http://www.dickblick.com/lessonplans/pdfs/japanese_lanterns.pdf

Incredible Art Lessons: *"Art of Japan:"* http://www.princetonol.com/groups/iad/Files/Cathy-Japan.htm

Richie, Donald. *A Taste of Japan: Food, Fact & Fable; What the People Eat; Customs and Etiquette.* Tokyo, New York, & London: Kodansha International, 1985.

Scott, David. *Japanese Cooking: Pure and Simple.* New York: Exeter Books, 1986.

Shimbo, Hiroko. *The Japanese Kitchen: 250 Recipes in a Traditional Spirit.* Boston: The Harvard Common Press, 2000.

Steinberg, Rafael, and the Editors of Time-Life Books. *The Cooking of Japan.* New York: Time-Life Books, 1969.

Further Reading

On the Internet

How to Make an Origami Crane
    http://monkey.org/~aidan/origami/crane/index.html
Japan 101—Japan Information Resource
    http://www.japan-101.com/
Japanese Sumi-e Painting
    http://www.international.ucla.edu/shenzhen/2002ncta/lindemulder/
    sumi-e.html
Japan's Ministry of Foreign Affairs: Web Japan
    http://web-Japan.org/index.html
Kids Web Japan
    http://web-japan.org/Kidsweb/index.html
Origami Resource Center
    http://www.origami-resource-center.com

Glossary

arable (AYR-uh-bul)—Land that is suitable for farming.

boil (BOYL)—To heat a liquid until it bubbles.

broil (BROYL)—To cook food, such as meat or poultry, under direct heat.

Buddhism (BOO-dih-zum)—A religion founded in the sixth century BCE in India by Siddhartha Gautama, known as Buddha, "The Enlightened One." Introduced from China and Korea in 552, it is Japan's major religion. Of Buddhism's numerous sects, it is Zen Buddhism that has most influenced Japanese culture.

calligraphy (kuh-LIH-gruh-fee)—Handwriting as a fine art.

dashi (DAH-shee)—A sauce made of dried kelp (seaweed), fish stock, sugar, and soy cooked together and used as the basis of many Japanese recipes.

geisha (GAY-shah)—A woman trained from girlhood in dancing, singing, and playing the *samisen* (a stringed instrument), as well as formal etiquette and the art of conversation, in order to entertain men.

kimono (kih-MOH-noh)—A robe with wide sleeves, often made of silk, that is the traditional dress of both men and women in Japan.

lacquer (LAK-ur)—A protective coating made from the sap of trees that is applied to seasoned wood.

lathe (LAYTH)—A machine used for shaping cylindrical pieces of wood.

marinate (MAYR-uh-nayt)—To soak meat or poultry in special sauces, spices, and fruit for a time so that flavors soak into the food before it is cooked.

mochi (MOH-chee)—Sticky rice cakes made of cooked white rice that are pounded into paste, then formed into cakes and usually broiled or baked.

ocha (OH-chah)—Green tea, which begins and ends nearly all Japanese meals.

onigiri (OH-nih-geer-ee)—Cooked rice shaped into balls and wrapped in dried seaweed, usually with smoked salmon or pickled plums inside.

Oshogatsu (oh-shoh-GAHT-soo)—New Year's, celebrated for three to five days; Japan's most important holiday.

samurai (SAM-ur-eye)—Members of the military class in old Japan.

sauté (saw-TAY)—To brown meat or vegetables with a little butter or oil in a pan or wok on top of the stove.

Shintoism (SHIN-toh-ism)—Japan's earliest religion, it focuses on honoring nature, one's ancestors, and ancient cultural heroes. The eight million gods who make up the Shinto pantheon are honored with offerings of rice, fruit, and vegetables at village shrines and temples throughout Japan.

shoji (SHOH-jee)— Sliding panels of rice paper on wooden frames that are used in Japanese houses, inns, and temples as windows and doors or as partitions to separate rooms.

simmer (SIH-mur)—To cook slowly over low heat, without boiling.

soba (SOH-bah)—Thin noodles made of buckwheat and eaten either hot or cold..

sumi-e (SOO-mee-a)—The art of painting ideographs and pictures with India Ink, made from black sticks of soot, mixed with glue, and dipped in water.

tatami (tah-TAH-mee)—Thick mats made of woven rice straw.

tokonoma (TOH-koh-NOH-mah)—An alcove in a Japanese house, usually near the front entrance, where seasonal flowers and other beautiful objects are placed. A hanging scroll, or **kakemono** (KAH-kay-MOH-noh), made of silk or paper, with dowels at top and bottom, usually exhibits a seasonal picture.

Index

ABOUT THE
AUTHOR

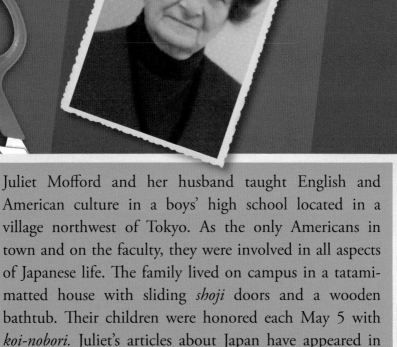

Juliet Mofford and her husband taught English and American culture in a boys' high school located in a village northwest of Tokyo. As the only Americans in town and on the faculty, they were involved in all aspects of Japanese life. The family lived on campus in a tatami-matted house with sliding *shoji* doors and a wooden bathtub. Their children were honored each May 5 with *koi-nobori*. Juliet's articles about Japan have appeared in the *Boston Globe, The New York Times, Christian Science Monitor,* and *Scholastic Teacher.*

"Japan was the highlight of our professional lives," Ms. Mofford says from her home in Maine. "Teachers are highly respected there and students, eager to learn!"